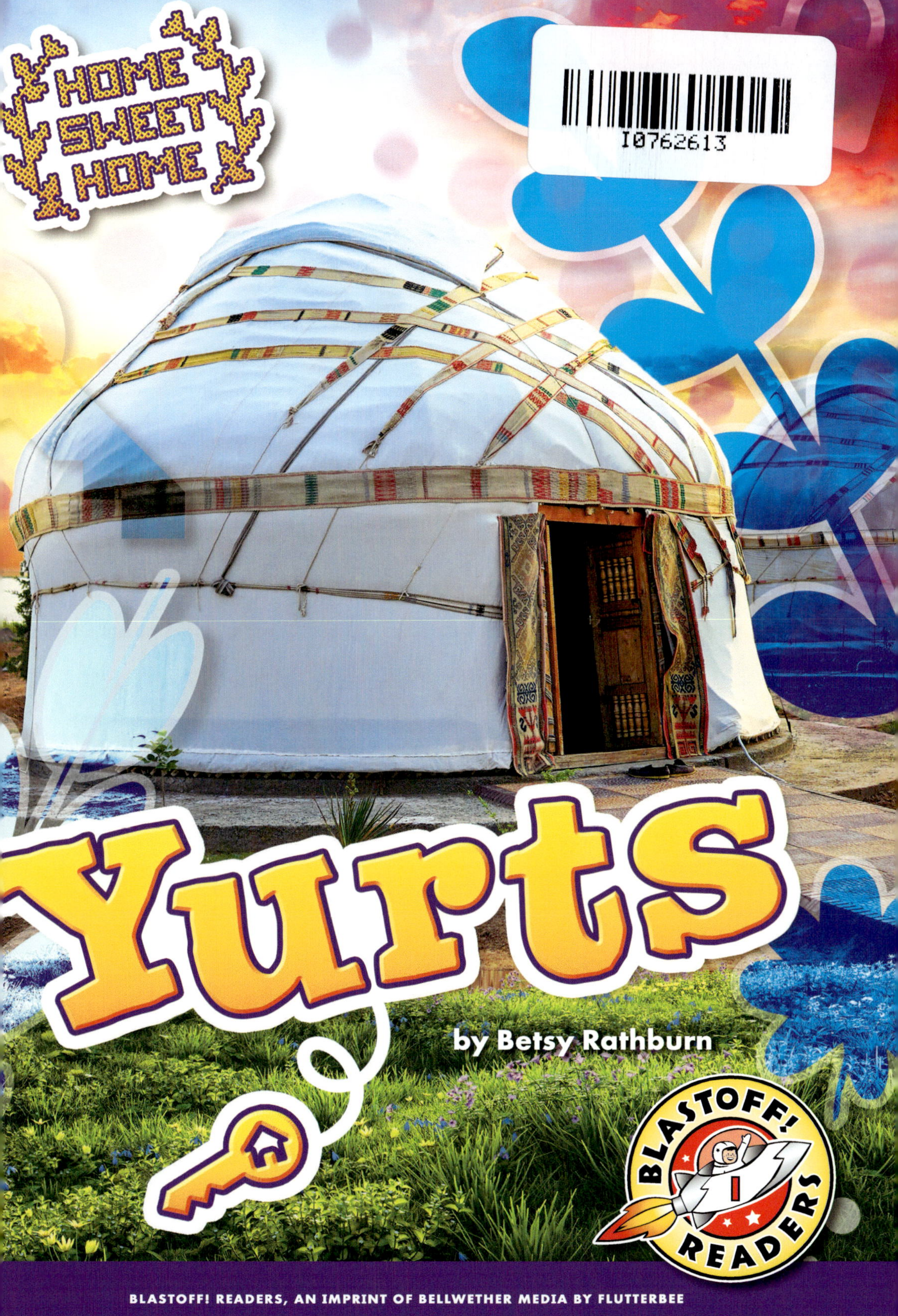


BLASTOFF! READERS, AN IMPRINT OF BELLWETHER MEDIA BY FLUTTERBEE

**Blastoff! Readers** are carefully developed by literacy experts to build reading stamina and move students toward fluency by combining standards-based content with developmentally appropriate text.

**Level 1** provides the most support through repetition of high-frequency words, light text, predictable sentence patterns, and strong visual support.

**Level 2** offers early readers a bit more challenge through varied sentences, increased text load, and text-supportive special features.

**Level 3** advances early-fluent readers toward fluency through increased text load, less reliance on photos, advancing concepts, longer sentences, and more complex special features.

★ **Blastoff! Universe**

Reading Level

Grade
K

Grades
1–3

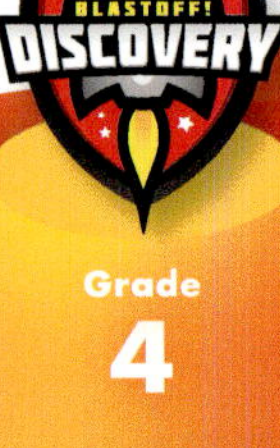


Grade
4

This edition first published in 2027 by Bellwether Media, Inc.



For information regarding permission, write to Bellwether Media, Inc., Attention: Permissions Department, 3500 American Blvd W, Suite 150, Bloomington, MN 55431.

Library of Congress Cataloging-in-Publication Data is available at www.loc.gov or upon request from the publisher.

ISBN: 9798898800321 (hardcover)
ISBN: 9798898802851 (paperback)
ISBN: 9798898801564 (ebook)

Editor: Rebecca Sabelko Designer: Andrea Schneider

Printed in the United States of America, North Mankato, MN.

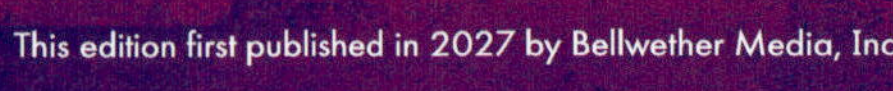

# Table of Contents


Weekend Stay 4
What Are Yurts? 6
Inside a Yurt 12
Glossary 22
To Learn More 23
Index 24

## Weekend Stay

We are visiting a state park this weekend. We are staying in a yurt!

# What Are Yurts?

Yurts are round tents. They are **portable**. They can be moved anywhere!

People in **Central Asia** first used them. Now they are used around the world.

Yurts are made of wood and **fabric**. They can be built fast!

# Size of a Yurt

1 school bus

1 yurt

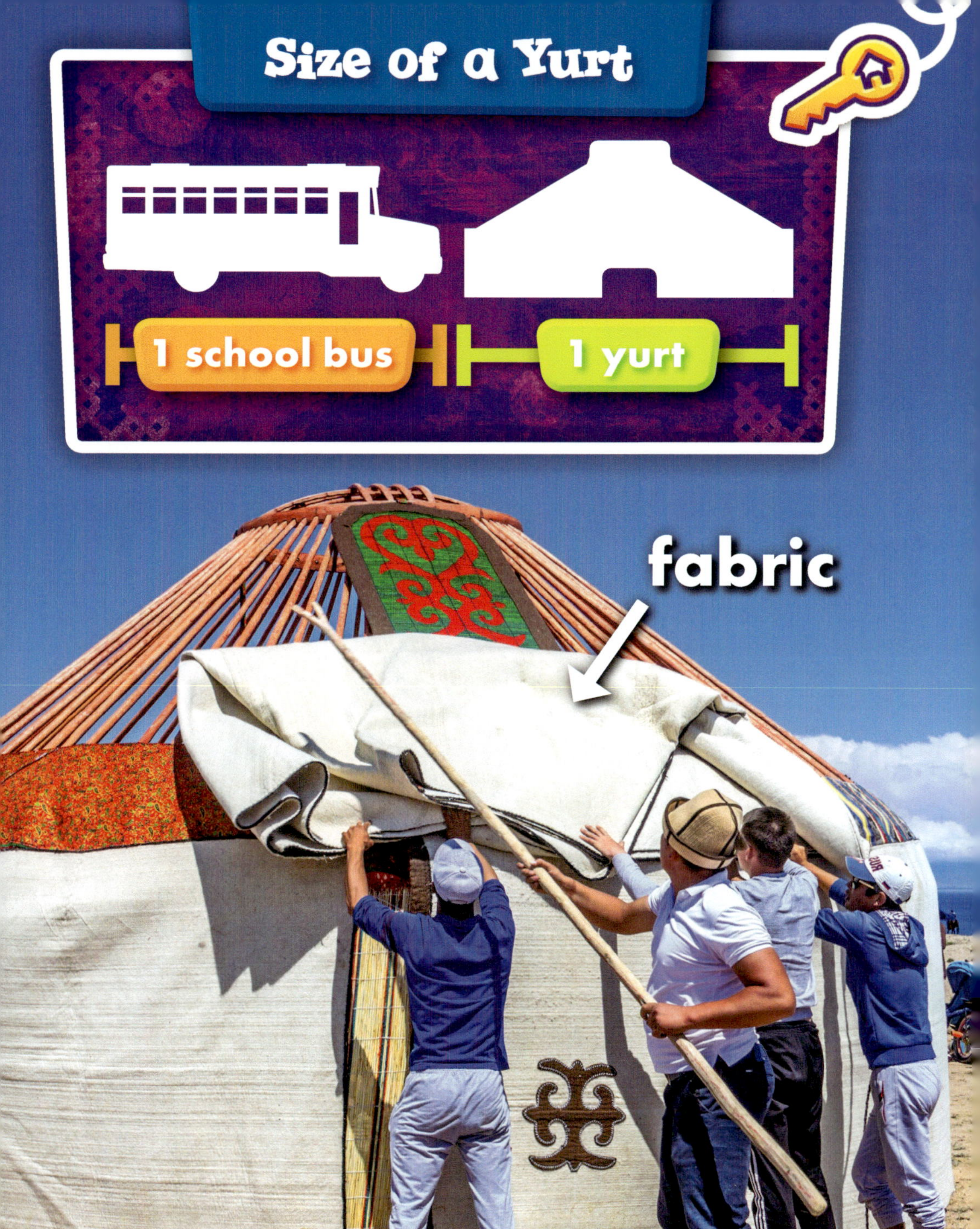

# Inside a Yurt

A yurt often has one big room.

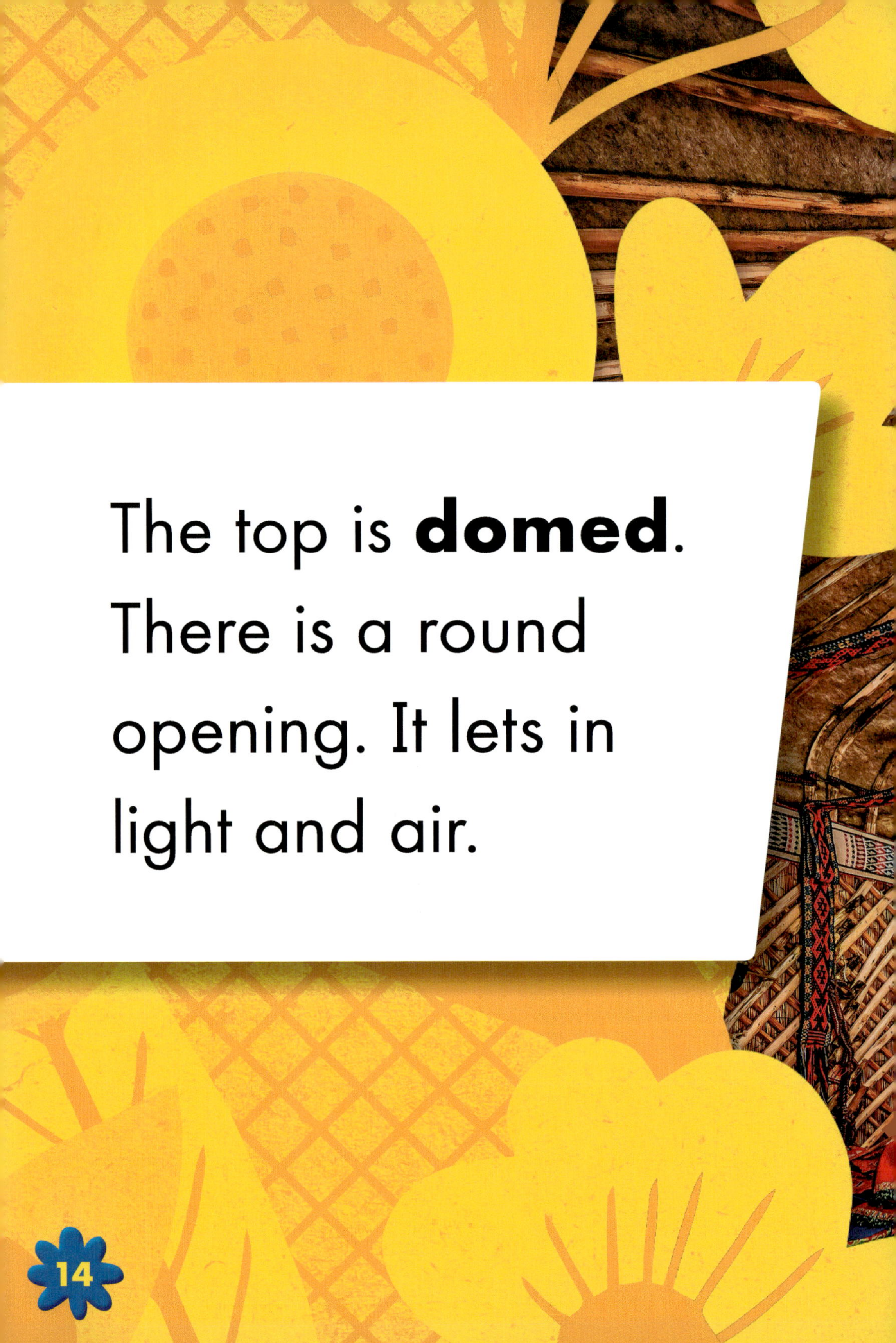

The top is **domed**. There is a round opening. It lets in light and air.

domed top

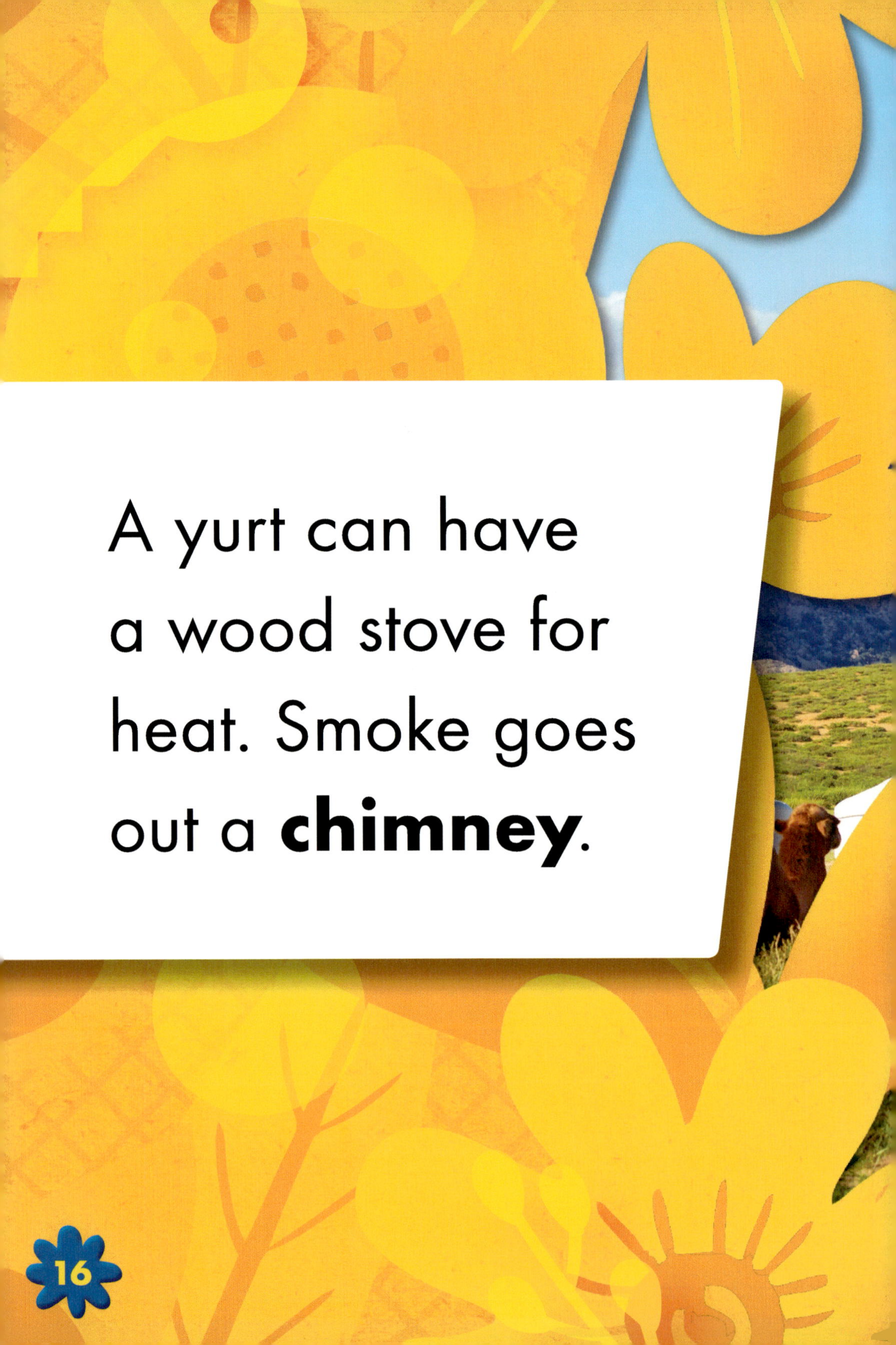

A yurt can have a wood stove for heat. Smoke goes out a **chimney**.

wood stove
chimney

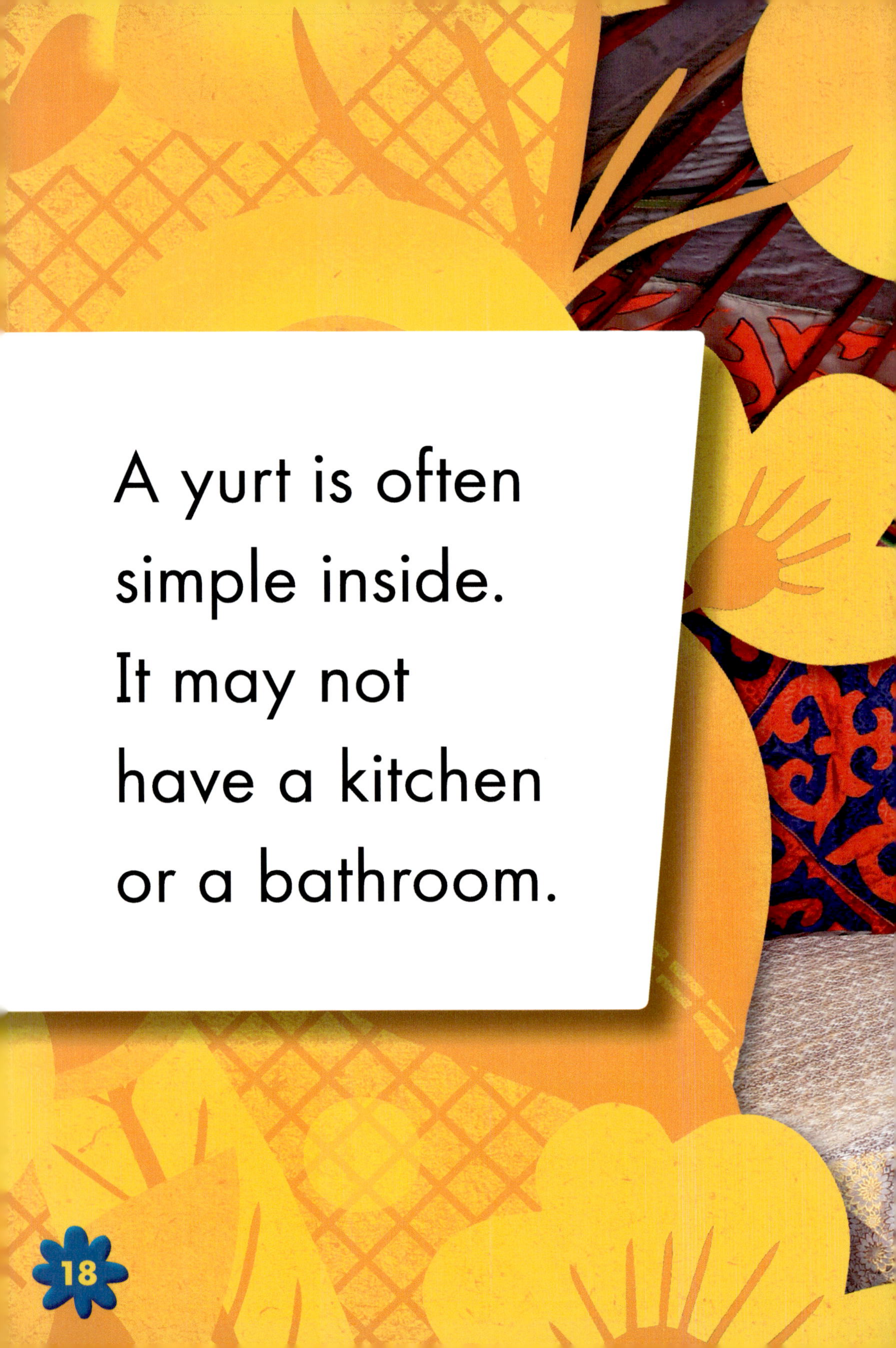

A yurt is often simple inside. It may not have a kitchen or a bathroom.

# Parts of a Yurt

These homes
are built to move.
They are **unique**
places to live!

# Glossary

**Central Asia**

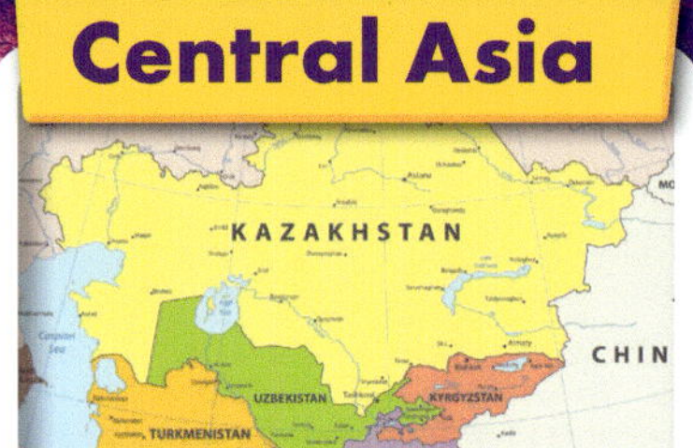


an area in the middle of Asia

**chimney**

part of a home that lets out smoke

**domed**

rounded

**fabric**

a type of cloth

**portable**

able to be moved easily

**unique**

one of a kind

# To Learn More

## AT THE LIBRARY

Lawrence, Ellen. *Homes Around the World.* Minneapolis, Minn.: Ruby Tuesday Books, 2025.

Rathburn, Betsy. *Igloos.* Minneapolis, Minn.: Bellwether Media, 2027.

Yomtov, Nel. *Asia.* North Mankato, Minn.: Capstone Value Library, 2026.

## ON THE WEB

**FACTSURFER**

Factsurfer.com gives you a safe, fun way to find more information.

1. Go to www.factsurfer.com.
2. Enter "yurts" into the search box and click 🔍.
3. Select your book cover to see a list of related content.

# Index

Central Asia, 8
chimney, 16, 17
fabric, 10, 11
parts of a yurt, 19
size, 11
wood, 10
wood stove, 16, 17

The images in this book are reproduced through the courtesy of: Aleksandr Lupin, front cover; Delphotostock, p. 3 (stove); ahmad, p. 3 (rug); Heidi, pp. 4-5; Nokolay N. Antonov, pp. 6-7; Maxim Petrichuk, p. 7 (inset); Pierre Jean Durieu, pp. 8-9; John Rodgers, p. 9 (inset); Matayas Rehak, pp. 10-11, 22 (fabric); Edwardje, pp. 12-13; Matthias Rhode, pp. 14-15; Vera Larina, p. 15 (domed top); pop_gino, pp. 16-17; Michael Sheridan, p. 17 (wood stove); Mikhail Mun, pp. 18-19; POUSSINFRANCAIS, p .19 (parts); MachineHeadz, p. 19 (wood stove); in4mal, pp. 20-21; Iryna, p. 22 (Central Asia); son of sun, p. 22 (chimney); Dina Lukoianova, p. 22 (domed); THP Creative, p. 22 (portable); Byheavens87, p. 22 (unique).